A BIRTHDAY GIFT

of

Poetry and Reflections

from

Patricia Batstone

ISBN 978 0 86071 852 9

Author Photographs:

Front Cover – *Jaffa meets Melvin*

Back cover – Top – *Magnificat*
Bottom – *Thomas Jones [TJ]*

CONTENTS

THE TIP OF MY PEN*

Lord, bless my pen.
May it always write the truth,
conveying only your love and will.
May it never be hurtful or vindictive,
neither unseemly nor frivolous,
or represent me in a false way,
even when conveying a lighter touch.
Rather, may it challenge, convict, comfort or encourage
those who need to see your Word for their lives.

Lord, bless my pen and bless this writer,
and together may we fulfil your work in the world.

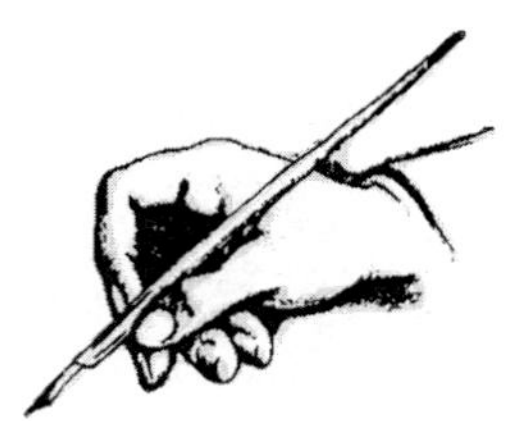

* Written at High Leigh, Hoddesdon, during an ArtServe Conference, based on words in *The Hymn of the Universe. Pensee 9* by Teilhard de Chardin who wrote: *There is a sense in which Christ is at the tip of my pen, my spade, my brush, my needle – of my heart and of my thought.*

INTRODUCTION

The possibility of becoming eighty did not please me one iota. The very mention of its imminence aged me as I clung to the things I could still do at seventy-nine – like chasing buses, cleaning floors on my hands and knees, climbing (increasingly modest) hills – and in and out of the bath for a shower!

I considered the purpose of birthdays other than celebrations and receiving presents – better still, surprises – as milestones in life: times to look forward for the young, and backwards when you're facing eighty. An excuse for nostalgia, for maximising the time left – and for **giving**. Not others giving to me but me marking the moment by giving to others – and what better way than by sharing, and giving thanks for, the one gift I was given at the age of thirteen when I made my Christian commitment. That event happened on Good Friday, 8th April 1955 as the result of a Billy Graham relay on the television from the Kelvin Hall in Glasgow. The very next day, eager to record the event, I began writing verses, and I just went on writing, and back at school I shared my writing as my way of passing the Gospel message on to my friends (not too difficult in the context of a very good Church of England village school). Several years later, travelling by train with my peers to our first jobs, it became a standing joke that I'd be happy if they gave me an exercise book and pencil for Christmas!

For me, poetry is a wonderful therapy, especially at times of illness, disappointment and restrictions such as those we faced during the Covid 19 pandemic. So much of my life, so many memories as well as thoughts and reflections are wrapped up in my poetry that when the idea of putting some of them together in a book to mark my advancing age, though without wishing it to look like an ego trip, I thought, why not?

I have no idea how many poems, reflections, prayers and other pieces I've written over the years – they fill dozens of A4 ring-binders. The question was, how to select a cross-section? First I thought in terms of subjects, but in the end I decided to present them chronologically – a way for me to trace my development as a writer decade by decade, limited to eighty pieces to reflect the number of years I've spent on this earth, and to those that have never been published, with the exception of just one ('Lord of All') which had appeared in the one and only edition of the school magazine and maybe an odd stanza here and there. Most of the earlier ones are too basic and evangelistic by my grown-up standards – the kind I would send back to the drawing board when I was involved in editing and publishing for others – so few have made the selection. I also seemed to have had a penchant for writing about death and dying – hardly the stuff of celebration! Inspiration came from many directions – from the contents of my mother's bookcase to the various jobs I've undertaken in my career. Those written for special occasions or that need explanation are accompanied by a short note. I have endeavoured to maintain a balance between what may be described as 'sacred' and 'secular.' There are significant gaps in the time-line. In the 'seventies I was occupied with gaining certificates and then beginning my time at university, so writing was confined to essays and dissertations. What I did write, as well as the majority of my work in the 'eighties has already been published. In the 'nineties I was also writing liturgy for books and journals.

So I invite you to accept and share these verses with my love and prayers that through them you may find enjoyment, inspiration, comfort, encouragement, or whatever is needful at this moment in time – and may God bless you in the days and years ahead.

Patricia Batstone

EARLY YEARS

LORD OF ALL*

God, my God, is Lord of all,
Of every creature, great or small.
He made every part of me,
And everything that eye can see.
He made the sun, the moon, the stars,
The Milky Way, the planet Mars.
He made the world o'er which to rule,
And then the sky, a starry pool.
He made the flowers, grass and trees,
The spiders, flies, and moths and bees.
He made the barley, corn and wheat,
The winter's cold, the summer's heat.
He made the earth on which we stand,
Made every object in the land.
And now he rules this Mighty Main
As Lord, in this, His Glorious Reign.

* Published in the one and only edition of the Long Itchington Church of England School Magazine, 1956

ECSTASY*

What is ecstasy?
A feeling of rapture?
Or infinity
trying to capture
something that isn't real?
A thought or a dream?
No! We mustn't steal
from things that only seem
to be; it must not be so.
No! Ecstasy is the feeling
of being loved and loving,
of proving
our every wish.
Rapture in reality
is ecstasy.

* From school I gained a scholarship for a commercial course at the Mid-Warwickshire College of Further Education in Leamington Spa. At one of our first English lessons (Shakespeare, I presume), the teacher asked the meaning of the word 'ecstasy' – and Miss Collins shot up her hand and cried, 'Rapture, sir!' The man was stunned and then asked this 15-year-old, 'And do you speak from personal experience?' He became my first literary mentor.

HEARTBREAK ON CALVARY

Women toiling, weeping, wailing;
women kneeling at his grave.
Women's cries to nought availing,
crying out their Christ to save.

Women knowing sadness, sorrow,
women knowing heartbreak;
still were they weeping on the morrow –
his death was more than they could take.

"Women! Women! Cease to weep!
Women, come and look to see
that watch you need no longer keep,
nor break your hearts on Calvary.

For Christ has risen from the deep,
returning from eternity."

A WORLD APART

I have toiled in a desert, sandy and bare,
Seeking oases that were not there.
I have battled in pain on a frost-bitten night,
Dazzled by snowflakes, blinding as light.
I have voyaged afar to be lost in a wave,
Tossed through the surf, washed up in a cave.
I have glimpsed the life unknown to man
That lies beyond in death's dreaded span.
I have felt love's touch, its tenderest bliss,
And known the thrill of a lost love's kiss.
In a single night I have conjured up schemes
That are lost to the light, and found only in dreams.

MUSIC IN THE RAIN

Have you noticed how much the birds sing every time it rains,
as the raindrops flow so gently down the window panes?
The rain-soaked leaves glisten as from tree to tree
the little birds with winged grace flit, singing merrily.

All the land's a radiant place when raindrops start to fall,
bringing fresh awakening and life into the call
that echoes from the tree-tops, the hedgerows and the grass -
the music of God's creatures no human can surpass.

Each melody blends softly with the gentle pit-a-pat
of spring and summer showers, their music meaning that
they feel the world is theirs, they are its only race,
even storm and thunder cannot hide their bounteous grace.

Though they sing throughout the seasons, no time can compare
with those melodious voices that charm the cooling air
when the rain has fallen gently from God's clearing sky,
and all the earth, refreshed, welcomes their joyful cry.

THE POET

It can be spring in winter,
Summer filled with autumn airs,
A Poet finds his pleasure
In a world of fantasy.
A memory that is bitter
Can be furnished without cares,
For the Poet in his leisure
Forgets reality.

The saddest song of love
Becomes a happy, carefree thing,
The wanton Poet's pen
Sets words on fire.
The very angels up above
Can shout aloud or cease to sing.
And what was sacred to him then
He casts into the mire.

In pathos and in beauty
He brings his pen to write.
The Poet, with a vengeance
Or meek deep in the heart.
It is his bounden duty
That he with all his might
Should conjure up such rank pretence
And play so cruel a part.

THE SILENT WITNESS

The Lord lit a flame of love in my heart,
And out I went to kindle a fire,
But the world was hard and would know me not,
For its people were wrapped in selfish desire.

Friends and relations would pay no heed
And my joy was transformed into dark despair.
But God in His goodness called me one night
As I knelt before Him and wept in prayer.

"Speak not, but go your way in faith,
A Gospel of works to all you must take,
As a silent witness,
Dumb for My sake."

With my hand in His I walked abroad,
Silently sowing His seeds of love,
Till the people I met began to search
And to find that wondrous peace from above.

Then the Lord commanded me take up my pen
And write of His praise for all to see.
Now, as in glory, His gift I employ,
I know my redeemer lives in me.

FOR SALE*

Our Father ...
    In Heaven ...
        Thy Will be done -

The face of Jesus,
Sadly pleading,
Gazes down from battered frame
On people
In an attic room
Battling to own
A pile of junk
At an auction sale.

Victorian ivy,
    Dull brown
        On papered walls

Accompanies the searchers
Down a flight
Of narrow stairs to second floor,
Bare,
Stripped of life.
Soft walls are harsh,
Floors are hard -
The sun shining through them lives.

Dust upon dust,
    Settled, unsettled,
        Settling again.

From bedroom to bedroom,
Stacked high with beds and
Mattresses:

Wondering constantly,
“Is this the room, the bed
Where spirit fled?”
Some strange sectarian spirit,
Wrenched to place unknown.

Lot by lot
The effects
Are willed from home.

Ornaments: exquisite, gaudy,
Modern, antique;
Paintings: oils, prints,
Country scenes,
Pastoral, tranquil;
Likenesses of splendid men -
The auctioneer's hammer
Dooms them all.

And books -
History books,
Books about strange places;

Of war, of peace,
Of poetry.
Famous words, infamous deeds
Hidden in pages
Yellowed with age,
Worn and dusty:
Two ancient volumes,
Half dead, they lived too long.

Pots and pans,
Copper kettles
Find new homes, new kitchens,

(Or are they destined to timely end
In some destructor's yard?)
The lots are sold,
Unsold -
People pay ridiculous prices
For rubbish,
Are broke
Pursuing bargains.

Feet trample
The Floors
Of stately home.

Gone her peace
Her floors laid bare.
The lots are cast
And she divided
Like Israelite spoil
Or Saviour's shirt.
Torn from her yesterdays -
Into tomorrow.

* One of my early positions as a shorthand/typist was with a firm of estate agents/auctioneers in Leamington Spa and I wrote this poem after my first experience as the auctioneer's assistant.

THE EIGHTIES

WALK FOR THE WORLD*

Walk for the World!
Setting out with our best feet forward,
We carry the message far and near,
Wearing our T-shirts, our banners converging,
One in a Cause we all hold so dear.

"Sign for the World!
We don't want your money, not even time,
Just your name on paper, your heart in support.
Don't be apathetic to brothers in need,
Try understanding; please spare them a thought."

Feel for the World!
In the heat of the sun we can quench our thirst,
Under lowering skies we increase our speed.
As the rain drenches we're made more aware
That water is half the world's greatest need.

Pray for the World!
When our journeys are done and the flags rolled away,
May we never forget that injustice goes on.
In bringing our plea to the eyes of the West,
May we never give up till our Cause is won!

* In June 1989 I participated in a Walk for the World from Gravesend to Dartford.

STUDYING THE MARKET*

Weary the garden path, press on the bell,
Authority brandished, the patter to sell:
"Good day! May I ask you
To give me some time, just a moment or two
To answer some questions about what you do,
The things that you buy, what you take to be true?
(It's my job, you see, to call door to door
And ask mundane questions you've all heard before.)
I've chosen you specially, you so look the part -
You're wearing your habits writ large, so I'll start ...

Now do you drink coffee, chocolate or tea,
Use this brand of petrol, or travel by sea?
Do you take sugar, eat cream cakes or snacks,
use fabric conditioner for the clothes on your backs?
Do you have central heating or live in the cold
And d'you put your money on 'Trident Gold'?
Of course, you watch telly, but not Channel Four
Because if you do I can ask you no more!

Yes, I know that I said it would take just a mo -
And half an hour later I'm still at your door,
But before I go, a few personal facts,
Like your age, occupation, and do you pay tax?
What was it you said that you did every day? -
A plumber, electrician, a master of play?
But I wanted a dustman, the man at the gate,
Or a millionaire in real estate!
And your age? - Oh, no, I have failed once more -
You only look thirty, not forty-four!"

Day in, day out, awake and asleep,
Trudging the streets my quotas to keep;
Two upper classes and two down below,
From one end of town to the other I go,
Drenched to the skin, raw to the bone,
Stifled in heatwaves, by hurricane blown.
There must be a better, more comfortable way
To eke out a living than hearing folk say
That they read *The Sun*, do the pools, watch the box,
Or the cat's having kittens, the children the 'pox,
And the world's in a mess and it's all the fault
Of politicians who need a jolt ...

What am I doing? Is this why I'm here,
To ask meaningless questions that aren't even clear?
I must have been made for better things
Like Frodo the hobbit in *Lord of the Rings* ...
So my mind spins off in a fantasy world
And the words on the papers are jumbled and blurred
And I want to be free of it all and be me ...
But first there's this tracker on camomile tea.

* While living in Gravesend I worked for a Market Research Company.

RED TAPE IN DOVER*

The white cliffs are shrouded in sun haze;
I cannot look over them to the sea beyond,
Only hear in the distance the gulls call
While the birds above me in the trees
chatter their tea-time chorus,
Loud even above the traffic hum.

And yet it is a picture of peace,
Broken only by the grim relics of one October night
When the fierce hurricane felled and uprooted history.
Red tape marks the spots
And the dead stumps and roots open up a view with breathtaking clarity.

So many greens shielding the dead brown broken branches,
Enhanced by sun-made shadows
Faintly ruffled in a soft breeze, or the spring
of happy birds on the leaves.
So much died that is forgotten.
So much lives.

* Written in Connaught Park, Dover the year after the devastating hurricane of 18th October 1987.

ROSARY WAY*

I walked the way of the Rosary,
Tracing a hope from birth to life.
'Hail Mary!' hung upon the air
As pilgrims paused at every shrine.

I stood and let my spirit drift
Along with theirs, till, unaware,
Harsh voices broke upon the air ...
This is a place of peace, it said.

A cigarette met me on the way,
Its odour spoilt the garden air
And seemed to desecrate the view.
The notice said, 'No smoke, no noise.'

The pilgrims, their orisons done,
Dissembled, laughing, by the shrine,
And backed by Joseph's bended knee,
Took their cheery photographs.

I let them go, retraced my steps,
Began again my journey there,
And silently, with book and pen,
I turned it into poetry.

* Written at Aylesford Friary, Kent.

KNOWLEDGE*

Bookshops ought to be made to give a bit away.
They can afford it.

What price knowledge?
Ninety-p for a Ladybird
When a few pounds more
would buy a treasury of words.
And with it the gaudy seventy-p card.
But books are so expensive now.

No tax on knowledge.
Books, food, headache pills,
all exemptions from a budget clause.
Read, eat, recover afterwards tax-free
and mark the page with Garfield's tasselled grin.
Someone's making a fortune out of books!

No discounts on knowledge.
No ten-percent out of the bookseller's till
without a licence to perform
the stunt of calculating how to raise the cash
to buy a VAT-ed video. Who pays the price?
The seller with her silent stores of unread knowledge.

They do not understand.
They have no knowledge
because they have no books.

* In 1988 I became the proprietor of a bookshop in Cullompton, Devon. This poem was written in response to some of the comments made by customers.

THE NINETIES

'MANNA!'*

A little thing it was,
packed and wrapped as though it were a precious gem,
some priceless ornament,
a crystal vase
or fragile clay.

It whispered with its being,
'Hold me carefully or I will break your heart - and mine.'
I couldn't touch it then
or see, for tears
loosed from yesterday.

A gift it was indeed, a present
brought as though from death to faltering life.
I hardly dared to breathe
lest this ethereal moment
slipped away.

And yet, it had to go, a fleeting glimpse,
past hope and future fear, a thread of gossamer
woven with such tenderness,
fashioned as a figment
of today.

* 'Manna' is a Hebrew word meaning 'what is it?'

WHOLENESS*

I went for a walk, seeking inspiration,
came to a gate with no way through
except to climb over it, into a field.
One field usually leads to another -
not this one:
it had just one way in, one out -
one whole field,
complete.

Every other way was blocked by barbed wire or blackthorn,
even the gilding corn crept over and barred the way,
and I thought:
This is wholeness!

The sounds of freedom stung my ears -
the hounds frantic in their barking,
the answering farm dog joined responsively,
The traffic hum, the trains, the trilling birds -
no human sound to intervene
where nature and materialism met.
And I felt trapped in the wholeness that was this field,
caught in its completeness.

The leaves swayed in the gentle breeze,
a rabbit scurried to a better shelter,
birds fluttered angrily in high branches.
I had disturbed their ease.
Every other sight lay in the distance
as sun and tiny spots of rain
vied for supremacy.

And I was trapped in clover and the dross
  of life under my feet -
Nature in completeness:
Whole.

And I thought: Is this like the wholeness of my life,
  fast bound, locked in,
  with no way in, none out?
No hope of others reaching out to me
  and I trapped in my own electric fencing.
An early butterfly fluttered into view,
  brief beauty, soon spent,
  and life became too precious to erect such barriers;
  my wholeness was too taut,
  too concrete,
  too complete.

And then I saw it, almost where I started -
  the open gate, the footstool in the fencing.
I saw what I had not seen because
  I had turned my way,
  made my own assumptions,
  mapped my course.

It was a whole field still,
  but this time, too,
  it seemed complete in having exit, entrance,
And I was free - I thought - until I turned,
  and coming into view,
  one of God's creatures made it plain
  that I had trespassed into her domain,
  and she was right, of course, in what she did:
Wholeness has its boundaries, after all.

Written at The Hayes, Swanwick while seeking inspiration for the Methodist School of Fellowship 'Revels'.

APACHE GOLD*

O Geronimo, as you look up from your uncertain grave
And see your children clamouring in the cold,
Are you proud of Cochese now
Who sells their souls for white man's gold?

They came once with guns and writs,
Hungry for your glittering land.
You were an obstacle, a scar, and had to go:
You locked your heart and took your stand.

O Geronimo, Geronimo,
Did you weep for your children then
As Rachel wept
Because they were no more?

They took your freedom then,
For when they could not wipe you out
They herded you to 'reservations,'
Offering uneasy peace: "So do not shout

Abroad that we are madmen
Only out for power and wealth.
We're settling you in safety now,
We're offering life and health."

O Geronimo, Geronimo ...
Do you weep ... now?

They come today with videos and promises,
Offering riches in contaminated crust -
A glowing future, security - and risk:
To sell their souls for white man's dust.

This earth, your earth, a landscape green, though poor,
Becomes a black repository
For what the greedy world discards -
Tomorrow through eternity.

And what will be the price they'll really pay
For this fine fuel of tomorrow's fire
That reaches the horizon's orange glow,
Prepared and waiting like a funeral pyre?

What if some mad half-crazed antagonist
Should make one tiny puncture in a drum,
Or some unthinking sleepy operative
Lose one small screw beneath his thumb?

O Geronimo ...

* Comment on the news that the Apaches were selling land to be used for dumping nuclear waste.

DAWN OVER DAWLISH*

The hens have already gathered,
Chucking quietly out of the dimness,
Awaiting cock-crow,
The crude clarion call
Heralding a late dawn.

Light streaks the opening sky,
Whispers of cloud scudding into sight,
Precursor of dayglow.
In the still dampness underfoot
Hope is newly born.

Out of the grey/green mass of nature,
Almost camouflaged from view,
The peaceful tower rises,
Magnificent as the dark starling cloud
Which soars, screams, circles overhead.

Follow the faithful to the Feast,
Across the bridge we stand on holy ground.
A light surprises -
Reveals the Supper permanently pastelled:
Bread and wine, on altar spread.

Christ calls, not only to remember him
In images of bread and wine,
But, following their Lord,
As Jeremiah heard the voice, Break down and build, uproot and mend,
The faithful answer now.

Green and gold, brightly catching eye,
In unison His people stand
To hear the Gospel Word:
Come, follow Me, lay down your nets, set sail upon this
human sea;
Your Lord is in the bow.

In tune with Gregory and other saints
The course is set, and strength is given
In Bread and Wine,
To greet the brightness of the day, a blessing on each head:
May light perpetual shine.

Lamb of God,
... Grant us your peace
Along your chosen way.

* Written at Dawlish Warren, where I was participating in a Counselling Course, following a walk to St. Gregory's Parish Church for 8.0 a.m. Communion.

THE STONES LAUGHED*

The Stones laughed
when they saw us coming,
arranged themselves as
stumbling blocks
for untried feet,
shifting position at random.

They littered our way
as we walked -
together - distanced -
by stream, in fields,
protruding haphazardly
out of the pathway.

We travelled silently
in the rough shade,
each aware of other's pain
and own despondency.
We could not join the Laughing Stones:
life had no humour then.

When we spoke, hurt
rose to our lips
but we failed each in
understanding other's grief.
The Stones stared out in brightness,
scorning vacant promises.

Climb, climb. The Stones
gave tenuous foothold on the way;
listening to the thudding
of our tired hearts,
louder, louder; yet the
Stones laughed louder still.

The sun blazed down on aching heads,
the ground rose, scorched to burning feet;
caught in light, shade,
swamp and ditch,
we toiled - together - apart -
and in our agony of silence
the Stones were thunder in our ears.

It seemed all nature had conspired:
sheep, cattle, Stones and rain
made hazard of our path.
Trees shifted shade, water
dripped and oozed to muddy sludge
while laughing pebbles danced into our shoes.

The Stones laughed when I slipped and fell,
ducked in the running stream, left
damp and sore
while Mother Daisy
quizzically looked on
maintaining guard till all her field lay safe.

At last, the final stile!
A running brook with firmer steps to cross;
hour after hour now led us there to ask,
Can these Stones live,
turn into bread or scones with cream
for one missed tea?

*Written at Exford after walking The Exford Way on Geoffrey's birthday – an outing that didn't quite go to plan!

WELCOME TO EXMOUTH!*

I remember this view,
    out across road
    and railway,
    sand and mud-flats,
    out to the sea
    and the railway,
    the road,
    white houses dotting 'the other side'
    and the patchwork hills
    ascending to distant woods,
    deeply green in a grey distance,
    against a watery sky.

So little change, except
    the grassy bank
    fronting my view.
    Then there were daffodils,
    yellow blooms
    smiling in sunlight,
    closing at dusk,
    bent in the rain,
    haphazardly picked
    by passing tourists
    unappreciative of the need
    to leave them there.

Now to the bare green grass,
    trodden under weight
    of endless rain,
    dead foliage strewn in clumps,
    bedraggled among the living

sunlight streaks,
life comes, is given:
Ginger Tom glows as a monarch
resplendent in gold; camouflaged,
a finch hops from blade to blade,
and drawn by February's rays
two daffodils come to bud.

* Written at 'Peace Care', Exmouth. As the train drew into Exmouth Station spring visitors were greeted by 'Welcome to Exmouth' outlined in daffodil blooms. This poem was written from the other side of the bank that struggled to compete.

THE QUESTION MARK*

I watched the squirrel burying its nuts,
a deep question mark forming in my mind:
how, when the winter sleep is past,
will that same store be found?
It seemed a thing most wonderful
that such a tiny creature had no care
but busied itself prioritising need -
and detail done, it scampered off
to play another round,
delighting large humanity
made softer by its presence there.

* Written in Kensington Palace Gardens.

THE WEARY DEVON FARMER

Night came, the farmer went to work.
As dusk turned to dark he plied his task,
Made hay, ploughed his fields,
Sought and fed his cattle.

Night turned to dawn and he rested,
Weary of labour, poring over books,
His brain addled by figures,
His heart heavy with shortfall.

Dawn became day, the sun rose
And he looked longingly into its warm beams.
This was the price of progress,
The cost of roof and bread and coat.

Sunshine turned to sunset, red streaks on cloudless sky;
His day's labours done, he turned to the night's
As a soft birdsong fell onto hushed air
And put new thoughts into his tired mind.

Sunset sank out of sight as he gazed skyward,
Beyond the last red blur to distant clouds.
He reasoned with himself long and hard
That Nature slept while he worked on.

Dusk devoured day as reason reached its height:
Nature sleeps its full night span
And still fulfils what God requires,
For everything is balanced in His hand.

Dawn broke, crashing into his world with vibrant noise.
He stirred, then rose to find himself refreshed.
The day ahead stretched out its welcome arms
And he stepped out, his energy renewed.

HEAR THE SILENCE

Hear the silence -
The imperceptible calm in the Babel of noise,
The split second pause in the rushing time,
The moment when the world stops
for me.

Hear the silence -
The slow breath expelled from the heaving chest,
The heightened temper in the surging blood,
The long sigh of life in a turbulent world
in me.

Listen to the silence -
Nature hung in the balanced breath
Of a lamb's paw in play, the horse's stare,
The dog's ear tuned for sounds unheard
by me.

Experience the silence -
Deep in my human heart, in the dispeace
Of my existence, at the nerve ends
Of understanding, the pitched inner battle fought
in me.

Cherish this silence -
Brought by the Spirit's coming into life,
Disseminating peace in a broken world,
A knowledge unknown to Christless minds, flowing out
to me.

I am listening -
I hear the silence of my own thoughts,
Resting now, given as an offering to God
Who takes my gift, and, blessing, sends it back renewed
in me.

FETTERED SPIRIT*

"I wander ... lonely ... "
Not free, not even cloud-like,
but fettered to this weakened human form I long to rise above –
up, up where sun-play streaks the shadows through the trees,
and draws the squirrel early from his bed.

He is not free – nor I:
we are confused, together,
he frisking in bright daffodils from tree to river's edge,
the warmth deceiving him and teasing me apart,
tempting me with wonders my human eye evades.

I AM! I think – therefore I am;
this thinking, moving form,
complex as the wind that stirs among emerging hues
resplendent green and russet underfoot,
torn by fresh holly for another blood-stained crown.

Let me be free of this mute form,
that I may see, feel, experience, BE
the spirit life that is my patterning;
strip me of this frail mortality that hinders
dark rebellion brooding near.

I am a room, swept clean,
and into this wide open space there come
the darknesses that trouble human minds
and breathe the spell of evil into hearts
that hunger for excited Otherness.

Now I am free ... free
to wander at my pleasure through the earth,
disseminating madness in my wake,
living, laughing, livid on the foam cascading over stones
that send this human casing to its death.

And yet ... there is a darkness
and this vital feeling instinct now craves light:
starlight, sunlight, light of knowledge,
light that heals the broken spirit caught in time
and place; so near, but just one human heart away.

* Written at Meadhaydown, Dunsford

RETURN TO THE COUNTRY

In youth my country home was cold -
Blue breeze blocks
Hid behind experimental fascia
Miles from anywhere.

In marriage, country town provided
Standard semi. Bright blue and yellow paint
Softened a cold interior,
Snug on a new estate.

The city suburb called,
and life was good
And country colours, orange, green and warm
Shielded from non-existent northern gales.

To warmer climes, Kent township on a hill
Beyond a motorway.
Blue, brown tone to effect, neat and orderly,
Exuding peace behind closed doors of *Shadowland.*

It was the hope of better place to be.
When rural setting called,
We listened long
Then watched as life went drifting down.

Green was our colour, placid, cool,
Concealing all the stages of decay,
Masking rose-less alleyways
And rotting drains beneath our aching feet.

Now to a country hill we come at middle-age,
Modern, single-storey, power-stored and metered home,
Delight of hanging washing in a row,
Hearing cock-crow, hiding inconvenience
For joy in garden, garages and sills:
No country cott, but House of healing still.

THE GREAT COMMISSION

You said, 'Paint me a portrait, but not of you, or me:
    this one will need more thought, more detailed planning,
    it's not a subject for excitement any more.'

You sealed the subject in an envelope, made mystery.
    'This is the great commission;
    on this your future is at stake.'

And now, brush trembling in my hand,
    I face the meanest of impossibles:
    how paint such magnitude, unseen, unheard by human
        eye or ear?

Blake tried it once - great Architect, old man, stooped low to
        earth,
    but images cannot be plucked and handled –
    air, fire, breath of wind -
    nor yet that still small voice.

Perhaps a heart? Epitome of Love.
    But no: such love is cross-shaped, so I'm told.
    Or yet the God-man, manifested image - so he said.
    No, it's been done before.

Some object of exquisite worth
    that has no heart or breath
    could never lend itself to me
    to make the great commission real.

You say, how I procrastinate, reason like a legion at my call.
    No heavenly host, angelic choir or celestial wings
    shall kneel before my art:
    I have to say, I know my subject not.

But suddenly I see the smallest inspiration,
immense, it brings me to my knees.
I shall not paint a landscape, field or flower -
no - none of these;
instead, I'll paint a tear.

GOD'S TENDER TOUCH*

It comes with stealth,
that warm health-
giving touch
that says "I love you,
let me share your pain."

The message in my life replayed
Your proffered gifts displayed
invitingly,
saying "Come, and come again
to me
for healing rest
and resurrecting power."

* Written in the Army and Navy Store Café in London. This was the theme of the 1999 Women's World Day of Prayer when I took the service at Timsbury Methodist Church.

BLACKBIRD SINGING

The blackbird sang, it sang for me,
its high notes reached infinity.
It had no fear of man or beast,
while squirrels fled it gave its feast,
and yet a single magpie feather on
warned of some savage instinct on the run.

The blackbird sang, it sang for all,
as I walked on I heard its call
still ringing on the spring-fresh air
as I took time to give a care
to star-white flowerlets at my feet,
bright, growing in the sunshine's heat.

And all the noise of human fun
could never drown that blackbird's song.
It poured its heart and soul, so free -
I wanted to believe, for me.
But could it not, too, break its heart
and I would never sense the part?

For Nature has her therapy,
outstripping vain humanity,
which weeps and wails, bemoans its lot
yet for its neighbour cares no jot;
while out of every tragic clause
the blackbird still her music pours.

So I went on, by trees and stream
with sporting ducks whose helpless scream
pierced through the gentle blackbird's trill
until crude Nature had its will,
and only when I reached a cross
and chose the thunderbells, my loss.

Unregistered in this new sight
of carpeting so blue-flower bright,
but in another wooded shade
a trigger for my recall made:
a simple sign with memory shot -
a single blue forget-me-not.

* Written at Downend, Bristol

REACHING OUT

How comprehend the jumbled words which every now and
then
fill up my mind to bursting point and tumble from my pen,
to land in total disarray, scribbled as some vapour
on varied vacant spaces of reusable scrap paper?

I may select the nouns, the words that form identity,
give each a tense and verb to make immense activity,
add adjectives and after-thoughts to colour and confuse;
participles and pronouns perpetuate the ruse.

Then, too, the punctuation marks that separate each phrase
and pepper every discourse to make the meaning blaze:
stops, colons and apostrophes, plus commas by the score -
misplaced, they turn to falsehoods, throw discretion through the
door.

But if I do not listen to that whispered note and pause,
to the subject and the predicate, the construct and the
clause,
I shall find my fumbling efforts have led by wit to stray
and rendered wholly meaningless the truths I would convey.

What price the ancient sages with their tables made of stone,
the cave-men with their pictures, communicating tone;
Egyptian hieroglyphics, symbol, sign and note?
How far on we've travelled from learning all by rote!

Oh, folly that would strain so to capture every gnat
when often such a simple phrase conveys the stage we're at.
To feast on dictionaries, with photographic mind,
can't compensate a lonely heart for one word that is kind.

A POEM FOR PENTECOST

The Spirit moves,
spreading His wings of power over His careless world,
lighting flames in the dark crevices of human minds and
    hearts,
breathing a warming air into the cold abyss of feelings,
hovering in the thick mists of consciousness,
guiding our way through the dense fog,
moving again
in me.

And will He also give me language,
that I may express that inmost knowledge of His presence,
helping others seek Him, know and feel Him, too?
What mystery is this that steals my heart,
that takes my very breath away
and yet assures I am forgiven
who once forgot, ostensibly denied His moment of self-
    giving?
How am I blessed, who know His breath in me,
feel raptures of emotion, joy in being free
to live and love, be one with Him,
yet still be me!

The Spirit moved, and moving still
He spreads Himself across so vast a space,
and so is there in every drop of cooling rain,
the snowflake, hailstone, harshness of the sudden flood;
they speak of power in the smallest things
where He takes residence because He is so vast,
unfathomable; then the hastening wind,
warm breath, dries up the mire and creeps into my lungs,
a soothing, healing fresher air
that whispers 'peace.'

YOURS, FOR EVER*

Holy God, look now upon us,
make us want to be Your own,
teach us goodness, love and mercy,
be with us
for ever.

Son of God, be in us, round us,
fuse Your life and will with ours,
keep us free from earth's corruption,
make us Yours
for ever.

Holy Spirit, breathe in and through us,
purify our hearts and minds,
make us fit to be with You
and You in us
for ever.

Triune God, in awe and wonder
now we seek You as we are,
but when comes that great encounter
we'll be Yours
for ever.

* Romans 8:6-11

THE NOUGHTIES

THANK YOU FOR YOUR BLESSING*

You have blessed us, God, in every generation,
even when we have been undeserving
because of enmity with others
and towards You.
We thank You for Your blessing.

You have cared for us, God, through many years,
years spent doubting and denying You,
going our own way, looking to others
for the answers You alone could give.
We thank You for caring.

You have stood by us when we least deserved it,
when we preferred the company of Godlessness,
pretending to strength when we were weak,
paying lip-service to other gods.
We thank You for Your steadfastness.

Now, Lord, You will neither condemn us nor betray us,
for Your love compared with ours is absolute.
Help us to keep this understanding of Your love before us,
and may it enable us to praise Your Name
and to share You with friends and enemies alike.
We thank You for Your love.

* Numbers 23:1-12

UNMARKED GRAVES*

I visited you today.
You were so hard to find.
I needed help and he was kind, but,
having made the introduction, he walked away,
across your grave.

He couldn't have done that if one
had thought to mark the spot,
had found the little needed
to erect a simple monument that says
you're resting here.

What kind of rest?
The grandmother I never knew,
gone before your time, and mine;
and grandfather, alone, and suddenly.
Were you afraid, the way
your errant daughter feared her final days?

Days drawn out, days spent -
what?
Atoning?
She broke your hearts before you broke your own,
or hers.

Another unmarked grave enfolds the one
who lies, so near,
and yet so far away
you cannot reach or touch.
Is she, the innocent, beyond you now?

And here am I?
Bereft, yet mourning more for you, long gone,
because I could not find your resting-place.
Shall I now mark it?
Will you permit me serve you thus, the dead,
by dead neglected long in time,
till now?

* Written in Hartlepool after visiting my paternal grandparents' grave and that of my father's infant sister, all unmarked.

THE BLOOD-RED RUBY

It is a mystery how the paths of life
criss-cross and cross again,
some brought together, fused
and left to grow as one, the passing years
embellishing the seam into invisibility.
Others divide, return, divide again,
depositing new riches, thoughts, experience,
reforming friendships, merging memories till
the years fall full away; lost to our sight,
past and present are as one
and time stands still to count the future days;
months turn to years, and decades pass like gems -
the blood-red ruby, diamond specked,
uniting dreams and bright reality.

* Written for inclusion in a friend's Ruby Wedding Album

THIRTY YEARS ON ...

Thirty years, thirty years, thirty years on ...
Yet another birthday for my 'young' son.
It's hard to believe that yesterday's gone
and the battle for time is still being won.

Thirty years, thirty years, so long ago
welcoming Baby - how swiftly to grow.
Did we nurture a genius? How much did we know
that pen, notes and muse would soon start to flow?

Thirty years, such a time for a son to be born,
watching, and waiting, night into dawn.
And soon came the brush-strokes - and who might pour scorn
on 'Virginia's Garden' and artist forlorn?

But childhood has passed, and loneliness too.
The buds have all blossomed, and sparkle like dew.
Now the future so unknown stands beckoning you
while thirty years on, and all is made new.

* Written for my youngest son's thirtieth birthday. 'Virginia's Garden' was a whole room mural inspired by the writings of Virginia Woolf, painted at the Cottage Books, Cullompton premises.

MY HIDING-PLACE*

God is my hiding-place,
the shelter where I may pour out my troubles
and know the unseen shoulder,
the enveloping arms,
the hand brushing my hair,
wiping away the teardrops.

God is my security guard,
the one who clears the paths
and roots out the thorns,
the bracken, the unseen traps
that wound and maim
and suffocate a life.

God is my freedom,
the One who sets me free from prisons of fear,
of doubt and uncertainty,
the pride and arrogance of others;
then the walls I build myself
come crashing down.

*Psalm 142

MOMENTS OF INSPIRATION*

Moments of inspiration:
they come, like a thief, without warning,
or the spider, suddenly dashing from the curtain folds,
startlingly.
Like him, they may disappear without trace,
leaving an uneasy feeling
of not quite being alone.

Catch them if you can:
imprison them on paper, pristine white,
ruled, scrap, anything will make a prison
permanently
fixing, pinning down those children of imagination,
capturing as in a photograph
the briefest workings of a mind.

Now fashion them:
mould and knead and fill them with meaning,
pattern and unpattern, shape, reshape
unstintingly
until a work of beauty separates itself and says
"I am unique, my own identity
is stamped for ever on your thought."

So let them go:
let them live their life, reach out into the world
of time and space where they can fly
freely.
Only guard their perfection, their nuances,
against the plagiarisers, purposing to tunnel
through your lines of copyright.

*Psalm 45:1

TWENTY YEARS*

Just think! How twenty years have passed
since first you came to stay,
with all your life in one small van
ferried by a single man.
"It's not for long," you said.

Your goods and chattels thus disposed
or spread around in one lone room,
maintaining independence - but
so soon began our travels, space was cut -
"You'll have to shrink," we said.

Bit by bit props had to go -
the car, the wardrobe, half the tools
of trade you'll not forget.
Pace slowed awhile; it showed, and yet
"I'll not be beat'," you said.

In and out of hospital, losing your nine lives,
you've met each match that came along.
Alas! the stairs forced us to sell
and move out here to Dunkeswell:
"This will do me," you said.

So history came round again, back to the countryside,
and when you couldn't walk the block,
took to the pavement on three wheels.
Your ninetieth brought technology and all that it reveals:
"Best toy I've ever had," you said.

And now your anniversary's here,
near a quarter of your life
with ups and downs and much to share
these twenty years of growing 'care' -
"It's been a long, long time!" Who said?

* When my father moved to live with us in 1980 he declared it would only be for 'a couple of years'. 'No,' was the response, 'you're good for another twenty!' This poem was given to him on the twentieth anniversary of his arrival. He stayed for another three and a half years!

MILLENNIUM MUSINGS

The year is over. Was it an end or a beginning?
Was it the culmination of a lifetime's activity
or the precipice on which to construct an uncertain future,
reeling into Century Twenty-one?

What did it bring, this year of Jubilee?
Release from suffering for one,
but none for thousands sunk in uncreated debts,
no quarter for the homeless refugee.

A year of birth, a year of death.
Bouncing babies blest to loving homes,
a young life culled, snatched from the hearts
who'd laboured for his care.

A year of madness. Great endeavours.
Greater still the failures, successes dashed and shattered in
their wake;
a costly year, when planning turned to unreality
and hopes were washed away like dirty dreams.

Another year has dawned. Beginning or continuation?
The question dominates the theologian's mind,
while out beyond her brief the snow melts down
and earth begins spring warming much too soon.

Who cares? Who hopes for anything beyond their garden
gate,
each locked in worlds of might-have-been -
"I am all right - I've warmth and food and shelter -
I cannot contemplate it any other way."

Out there in the world's unspoken streets
are those for whom this day comes drear as any other,
except it isn't Christmas any more
and all goodwill's closed up and made for home.

We hide our eyes from cardboard shacks,
from crying children blind through our neglect,
from neighbours in far countries wracked with pain,
from all who'll never walk on earth again.

We turn and contemplate the date and promise to ourselves
that this year will be better: we shall strive
to speak out for the homeless, make them space
and give to those in need a sense of place.

But still that unseen conscience battles through
and says, "It's not enough! There's work to do
to make the world a better, safer place,
and however you shrink from it, that means you."

And now reflect: a year ago, high on millennium mania, did
we,
intoxicated by the media hype, spare one long thought
and ask what would HE do, whose birthday we proclaimed,
to bring a sense of justice, peace for all?

We made our resolutions then - life would be different:
we would love and care, move forward into time,
sow seeds of hope against the harvest of despair
now mouldering with the dross of 'ninety-nine!

Peace was to be the watchword - and still we speak,
but tones have dulled, the shout become a whisper.
The promised word we all resolved to bring
has floundered, and the bombs begun again.

Dare we once more make promises we know we'll never
keep?
Spread hopes and dreams before us each night before we
sleep
and say, "Tomorrow I will change the world"?
Tomorrow is a fickle thing: we know it never comes.

And so it is, we turn again to view the great unknown.
Our eyes are dimmed, our hearing dulled,
the years have ravaged us apace -
we live, and partly live, in need of grace.

What shall we promise, hovering on the brink,
how ratify our covenant with God, Lord of our time?
Perhaps it is much better that we simply kneel, and say,
'Lord, take my life, its promises, and make me Yours today.'

Written on 1st January 2001

HOLDING THE EARTH*

Holding the earth in my hand, small solid symbol,
its contours marked = the blue sea, land masses,
    a ridge of uncertainty within the order,
a fault line barely perceptible in the colourful perfection.

It is the ridge of uncertainty that becomes
    the cavern where evil lurks,
    where earth is poisoned,
    pollution festers deep inside, unseen, erupting,
        manifested in corruption and depravity,
        in living death.

It is the fault line that breeds infirmity,
    the sickness of injustice, scourge of poverty
    and human inhumanity,
and that once-rounded perfect earth
    is crushed and broken,
God-created,
    mechanistically destroyed.

But what is that to me, in my small corner,
holding this earth-resembling piece
of fractured glass?

Hold a pebble – smooth and marbled, pink and perfect.
Living within this fragile world of breaking glass
        - is this a pattern of my life –
or are its faults so barely visible
it can't be me?

The blue-brown stone is rough to touch,
    scarred and pitted, worn, washed-out its valleys,
    dulled its better parts,
and I identify.

This, like the marbled world is second-best,
    exposed to alien elements, abused, mis-used
    and fraught with problems –
ethereal, like the bubble floating on the wind,
    itself a whole creation, earth-shaped
    but fragile,
    waiting for the breeze to hurry it along;
    the first sharp gust of opposition
        shatters the illusion, like a wind, of change.

Who can take this earth, this living stone
and re-invent it,
form and fashion it and make a perfect
    pattern from the flow?

Only the hand that first created it,
    made it complete,
    a unity of purpose
    surging into Life –
Only the Maker: God alone.

* At a Methodist School of Fellowship workshop, held at The Hayes, Swanwick, we were invited to take an object and reflect on it, with emphasis on the environment. I chose a blue/white marble that resembled the earth as seen from space. It was read at the closing service of the week.

BOUND LAMB*

Still, silent Lamb, who bound you,
who strapped you with the cutting thongs
to make you bleed and cause you pain?
Who trussed you, live, like Sunday's chicken joint
and left you helpless on the cold stone floor?
Your smile betrays the pain,
your eyes anticipate a death
as you submit.

Was it some hired shepherd,
reneging on his task,
a pagan priest prepared for sacrifice,
the abattoir assistant sharpening his knife?
Or did you, with your mother's milk,
imbibe disease that snatches at your youth?
Has someone come with rifle in his hand
to send you on, to table or to grave?

Can you now hear your mother's plaintive cries
who sees the corpses piled, the smoke clouds rise
and knows by some rare instinct that
there'll be no shearing time this year,
no sheep-shorn paths
or gambolling in fields for lambs at play –
until you reach that great eternal pen
where no more harm can reach you, grass is sweet ...?

Meanwhile the earth and air are darkening now,
the stench of rotting carcasses and smoke
have filled your nostrils. Can you understand
that soon, too soon, those bonds will loosen in the flames?

Bound Lamb, your cries are silent, you submit –
you make us feel ashamed, we feel your pain
yet helplessly stand by and watch you die.
We do not see the Shepherd, waiting with his staff ...

Our vision stays with stark reality –
the blanket smoke, the funeral pyres,
the ropes that bind you tighter now.

* The inspiration for this poem came from the painting by Francisco de Zurbaran, 'The Bound Lamb' [*Agnus Dei*] which I encountered when visiting the 'Seeing Salvation' Exhibition in 2000. That painting inspired a whole raft of 'sheep' poems and reflections, some included in the book, *The Bound Lamb* [2013]. This particular one was written at the time of the serious foot and mouth epidemic of 2001 when thousands of sheep and their lambs were slaughtered and burnt.

THE HAND THAT CIRCLES TIME*

Each minute ticks away
another portion of my days,
the hand that circles time
ruthlessly pursues its course
          and will not let me go until
it is complete in me.

* Written at Dewlish Methodist Church, Dorset

THE BAPTIST*

Sharing, caring, watching, waiting,
unafraid to speak the truth -
here is one whose word is faithful,
dedicated from his youth.

His the task to clear the pathway,
his the servant, prophet role.
Humble, yet with confidence
points to one who makes all whole.

And with words that cause discomfort
he pronounces judgment clear,
yet the news is good to many
who still hold religion dear.

But the rich and powerful king
is not a man for one to cross -
and so the prophet's wings are grounded,
freedom stolen, people's loss.

Injustice cries throughout his prison,
stone and bars together weep
that one who talked of revolution
languishes, his head to keep.

But he still proclaims the Word,
the Spirit who will come and fill
the world with love and peace and pardon
when it stoops to seek his will.

* Luke 3:10-20

WHAT WORTH!*

His worth, a pair of turtle-doves -
not one, nor random two,
but paired to perfection,
one dedicated unit, born for progeny,
lives cut short for his life.

Our worth, a man upon a cross -
not any man picked off the street
but this one perfect Son of God,
dedicated to his Father's will,
sacrificed upon a rough-hewn tree.

What worth! When prophets see
a baby brought, his birth price paid,
and know this child the promised one,
the Light of nations,
Hope of all the earth.

What worth, when we, his followers,
face scorn and ridicule and harm.
Why should we shrink from suffering
when he has felt the nails driven in his palms
and borne the pain for love of us?

Such worth is more than precious stones,
a life of wisdom into power,
a life which wrestles down the years
embracing those who love him still
and take his hand in trust.

*Luke 2:22-40

THE FINAL RITE*

Out of the shadows they came,
two rich men, one with spices,
the other with a tomb.
Two men with clean-hands jobs
and dirty consciences
trying to make amends
by doing the dirtiest job of all -
the one no priest would touch
to avoid contamination.

Was it from love or guilt or duty
that they carried the Crucified
and gave a home to him in death?
And such a home! A garden tomb
set in a cave surrounded by the scent
of flowers and trees,
thrilled by the joy of bird-song,
at one with Nature.

They could have done no more -
unless they'd served him earlier
and used their wills to salvage him from death -
or was this meant to be?

And where, while these performed the final rite
were those who swore they loved him best of all?

*John 19:38-42

CONDUCTOR OF OUR LIVES*

Lord, You put music into our hearts and minds,
to soothe our stress and calm our cares.
You set the score, arrange the notes together,
tune Your instruments and then become
Conductor of our lives.
You measure chords and discords,
Your harmonies create the melody
and all the jumbled signs become
sweet music in our ears.
Each note is Your creation, matches mood,
slows us, speeds us, causes us to dance or sing,
make melody on instruments
and harmonise with You.
This is Your music, Lord,
Your rhythm, life-enhancing, totally affirming,
speaking love and beauty,
reaching out to height and down
to depths of ecstasy.

*Deuteronomy 31:19-21. Written in Wolverhampton while attending the 2002 Methodist Conference.

WHERE PARADISE?*

What riches have we in our store -
the treasured memories of life,
the little trinkets fondly given,
the souvenirs a snatch of heaven.
Such moments are for sharing,
bearing,
constantly repairing as the years increase.

Not gold and silver stored for rainy days,
or artefacts, the antique vagaries,
the might-be-one-day-valuable
detritus of living,
giving,
striving, surviving in life's battle-field
awaiting - what? A reckoning?

Count the moments, one by one by one,
each one a precious gem worth savouring
and hoarding,
applauding,
lauding for a future age.
Not tangibles or valuables but those things
well beyond the present age.

Back, back in time when life was young
and danced beside the Serpentine
and innocence stored up her magic hours
mistakenly believing,
leaving,
breathing, achieving that blest state
she thought would last for ever.

Life grows old - we reap the end
in pain and loss, in hope or desperation
until the final question rings its toll:
is that it, that all there is to human flesh?
Where is the treasured kingdom, where paradise?
Safe with far off memories,
nailed to a mouldering cross.

*Matthew 13:31-33,44-52. Written after attending the secular funeral of a very elderly neighbour and reflecting on some moments of her youth.

EACH OTHER*

When all the world's against us,
    I have you –
        You have me.
When no one else will listen
    I have you –
        You have me.

When the world seems sad and lonely,
    and the torrents tumble down,
when war and hatred threaten
    and nature wears a frown;
when joy is on sabbatical
and love has closed its door
    we'll never need to fret –
    for we'll still have
        each other.

* Written in Wirksworth for Valentine's Day 2006.

WALKING ON WATER*

Walking on water,
  treading the air,
    taking decisions,
      offering prayer -
        Lord, if you're there,
        help me!

Mission impossible,
  faith running short,
    trying to conquer
      niggling doubt -
        Lord, if you're there,
        show me!

Caught in the downpour,
  storm clouds close in,
    feeling I'm sinking
      deep into sin -
        Lord, if you're there,
        save me!

Holding Your hand,
  buoyed on the waves,
    now I am certain
      it's Jesus who saves.
        Lord, you **are** there,
        bless me.

*Matthew 14:22-33

NOTHING TURNED TO SOMETHING*

He was humbled - God raised him,
a slave, became our Master,
dead, yet still alive,
nothing turned to Something.

Sometimes the text is so familiar
we miss the point
the demeaning, bending low
among the dirt,

the foul feet of travellers,
hospitality of need
so subtly done -
a towel and a bowl.

And then the cross - he carried it for miles,
struggled, fell, was roughly pushed,
whipped and jeered at
while others sympathised

and one stood in his place -
a burly foreigner, picked on.
But only One could take the nails
and cry in victory.

And God exalted him, gave him a Name
that rent the heavens
and brought his glory back to earth
in human form.

*Philippians 2:5-11

I AM A CHILD*

Lord, I am a child, looking into your face,
barely aware of innocence,
waiting to be blessed.
I will not be kept away
even though the powers of separation
do their worst
and try to keep me from your Kingdom.

I am a child, lost in a big world,
searching for parenthood,
looking to be loved.
It is an elusive state
wanting to be part of your family,
secure and safe
in the folds of your eternal Kingdom.

I am a child, alone in the wilderness
of my own thinking,
longing to be free.
Trapped in my own mind,
my own interiority that craves
Your presence,
I feel you are too far to reach.

I am a child, about to go on a journey,
kneeling at your feet,
wanting to be absolved.
All my self-centredness
must be left behind, I know;
for everything I need
I'll find in you.

*Mark 10:2-16

ONLY THE MAKER KNEW*

See the clay,
ungainly lump barely pliable,
waiting the master potter's touch
to mould and fashion,
manipulate the mass
and from it work a miracle of life:
humanity -
tricked into being
by expertise Divinely engineered.

Who could have thought it possible
that such a complex race
might then emerge
from that one lump of clay?
Only the Maker knew,
the One who studied earth
who realised potential -
and when the light burned low
He sent a helpless baby -
nothing more.

Isaiah 64:1-9

MEMOIR FOR MAGNIFICAT*

You never changed -
age didn't enter your vocabulary;
Airs of feline perfection attended you,
your presentation,
that ecclesiology of grace
pervaded your whole being,
made you to love,
be loved
and trustingly accept we would forgive
the natural lapses of your state.

You were, so long, a presence -
there for me, for him
who needed your companionship
if not the evidence
of love misunderstood.
You knew how to appeal -
I taught you speech.
Each fleeting touch
brought ecstasies of sound.

You were incarnate innocence
shrouding cunning wiles -
we only guessed your motives,
but your needs were clear -
for doors, for food,
and for security
of knowing we were there.

Fastidious to the end,
well-groomed,
you posed the same way then
as you had done those sixteen years
of our delighting in your company.
Now you are gone,
yet not so far
as to be sought unknowingly.

You lie where you had found the perfect shade
in summer heat
or simply hid yourself from view
in private pain.
And still somehow I hope to turn
and find you sneaking up on me
or hear your silent hammering on the pane
or find you curled beneath a chair
or tucked in bed
or sunning in a border.

And when I come to earth
the questions rise -
could there have been a way
to save you from this grave?
What more could I have done
to tell you you were loved
although you knew
why there was no chastising,
open door, rapid departure -
you knew it all, who trusted me so much,
but did you feel betrayed?

* Magnificat [aka Nifty], so named because his previous owner was a Church Army Officer who went through the Prayer Book looking at all the 'cat' words when she rescued him from a factory site in Gravesend. As she couldn't keep him in a seventh floor flat, he came to us and became our beautiful ecclesiastical black and white cat. He died on 18th March 2003.

NO VACANCY*

One year on
the vacant spaces cry,
your sleeping places
silent now.

Still the drumming on the window pane
invisibly, since you are gone,
the hearing in my mind;
familiar sounds that once announced
your presence
becoming empty phrases.

Fleeting shadows of your ample form
are caught, and lost,
figments of illusion
and regret.

No reassuring brushes round my feet
engender harsh reality -
you're gone,
you're gone for ever.

The flowers by your grave bloom red -
only your garden corner
has no vacancy.

* Written in Dunkeswell on the first anniversary of Magnificat's death.

CELEBRATE A CENTURY

The world stood still a hundred years ago
to welcome you, new life among the old:
the future, like the summer sun, aglow.
None dreamt what different story would be told -

How life, so affluent and leisurely
if lived 'upstairs' - or harsh for those below -
would change; how hate and war destructively
would shatter peace, make innocence a foe.

A second revolution's culture shocks
would make your world much poorer in their way.
Long gone the pastoral shepherd with his flocks,
the horse-drawn carriages, and fearless play.

Yes, we remember pastures green and lush,
assurance that the world would never change!
But life cannot stand still; we grow, we rush
headlong towards each idol in our range.

A century on, can nothing still exist
of all you once held dear? Indeed it can,
for now you celebrate each turn and twist
with mem'ries no technology can scan.

So dream today, relive your yesteryears,
and count the precious moments one by one.
The past is gone, but only for those ears
that have not heard your music, shared your fun.

Yet how can any one of us deny
the progress we have seen and must embrace -
old hardships gone, though each day more slowly,
we are still runners in Life's Timeless Race.

YOU WERE THERE*

God of the Thin Places,
the gentle slither of space between earth and heaven
where whispered fears are voiced,
stories told and worries shared -
You were there.

God of the labyrinthine blue-brick paths,
the dizzying mystery of unprepossessing scene
that weaves towards the goal
and veers away, frustratingly,
You are there.

God of the destination,
the water bubbling up and playing down,
trickling, gurgling, splashing,
healing, cleansing life-enhancing,
mingling with the tears of penitence, release:
cathartic moments,
You were there.

* Written at The Hayes, Swanwick

THE BLUE TIN*

The tin was a gift -
    a blue tin
        filled with biscuits
            and a ballerina on the lid.
As a child, I coveted
    that tin
        that was a gift
        to Mother.

The tin, that was a gift
    remained upon the shelf
        biscuits replaced,
            the ballerina smiling still upon the lid.
As an adult I still coveted
    that tin
        that was a gift
        to Mother.

The tin was my bequest,
    the blue tin
        no longer filled with biscuits,
            yet the ballerina danced still on the lid.
A mother now, I filled the tin
    with cotton reels -
        part of the legacy that once belonged
        to Mother.

* Written during a Society of Women Writers' and Journalists' workshop held at the New Cavendish Club, London, on my sixty-third birthday.

A BIRD SANG

He came with the dawn
as the ice melted under a watching sun
and the cold air warmed
to his call –
that melodious song
that heralds spring
        - and life.

He sang as the first buds pushed their way
up from the wakening earth
and charmed the creatures
from their hiding place.
His song was filled with happiness
and all the joy
        of life.

And he sang through Easter parenting
and told a resurrection tale
that was his own,
still, but never silent,
a calling song that laughs at death
and brings to birth
        new life.

He sings again, today and every day
that time is short –
we, too, must watch and pray
and sing with him
the resurrection song,
then silently receiving
        life on life.

THOMAS COMES TO WIRKSWORTH*

I moved here from Ashbourne - in fact, I had no choice:
they put me in a prison car - the whole world heard my voice

because I cried and cried so loud the whole long journey through,
and when at last they let me go I was nowhere I knew.

It was indeed the strangest place,
carpeted and colourful with lots and lots of space.

But I have to say I tried to hide until I found
somewhere that I could feel secure away from human sound.

The food was good, but not a lot - I was obese, they said,
so put me on a diet, and watched me when I fed.

I looked out through a window and saw the distant plain -
Alas, for days and days on end they locked me up again.

One day I found an open door and made my bid for freedom.
There was a well-worn scented trail I followed: how I teased them -

hearing from a distance the frantic calls they made,
watching their activity as truancy I played.

But really I'm a wise old thing and know where I'm well in,
so condescended to return and settle down within.

By now I have the best of worlds - my own warm room by day
and when the evening darkness falls I can go out to play.

I also have some neighbours - Harry, Rosie, Domino;
as well as sneaky visitors whose names I still don't know.

Oh, yes, **my** name is Thomas Jones - known always as TJ.
I'm settling now in Wirksworth and hope I've come to stay.

* TJ was 'rescued' from The Ark. His name, which we interpreted as Thomas [Tom] Jones, came with him. He died of heart failure in November 2011 at the age of seventeen.

SIZE FIVE SHOES*

Size five shoes on size three feet -
My mother stood aghast,
but I had come of age, I thought
austerities were past.

Those shoes were white - they had to be -
quite flat, but long and thin;
I reasoned that their buttoned strap
would keep the spaces in!

So I, together with my friends,
set out one April night
to be confirmed, so we were dressed
from head to toe in white.

We reached the church a mile away,
assembled alphabetically,
veiled and nervously attent,
feet shuffling so excitedly.

Most wore white pumps so silently
they glided on towards their fate -
but my size fives were harsh and hard
clattering on the iron grate.

Then when I knelt they would not bend
preventing my retreat with grace.
Self-consciously, with head bowed low,
I tried to hide my burning face.

The walk back home was agony -
my size three feet had swelled to fit
those noisy boats I'd coveted
against my mother's seasoned wit.

High heels, stilettos, 'winkle-picks' -
I've borne them all with pain,
but never since that April day have I
worn size five shoes again!

* Written for a competition on the theme of 'footwear' and based on the event of my confirmation at Long Itchington Parish Church, April 1956.

THE POWER OF THE PAIR*

My boots were made for tramping
through swathes of virgin snow -
I didn't want to buy them but
they wouldn't let me go.
They were an impulse purchase -
they tempted, drew me close:
their colour was appealing -
a stylish shade of grey.

They had a British label
that told me they were 'K'.
I wanted to resist them -
it was so much to pay -
but their beauty so beguiled me
I couldn't turn away.
I met them in High Holborn
and took them to Gravesend.
They seemed too good to wear then
but like the truest friend
they waited quietly patient
for the day when their true purpose
would meet my desperate need.
Once I'd have sooner died a death
than dressed up in snow boots,
but such the power of this pair
that year by year at winter ice
they'd lure me out again,
to Sunday church or shopping spree
or errands round the town.
These twenty years they've carried me
and never let me down.
I'm glad now that I met them
and succumbed to all their wiles.

Now we tramp the snow together
and fill the world with smiles.
They've served me now so faithfully
I'll never let **them** go.

* Written for the same footwear competition. Those boots are still in service in 2021 and have cost me precisely £2 in repairs!

ACT OF BIRTH*

All our yesterdays, gathered into service,
linked with names and generations
long forgotten -
history given flesh and blood, and named.
And the spirit of the past links present,
future -
all combined in one momentous act
of birth.

And through the generations history
has punctuated lineage, sold it short
and taken in their prime
so many sons, much pain and heartache -
or life was so cheap that always
there were more -
until there came that one momentous act
of birth.

Son by proxy, king and yet
His coming was the lowest of the low,
rough-hewn
His birthing stool, the cradle where He lay,
His company the beasts of farm and field
carelessly watching overhead
when came that one momentous act
of birth.

* Matthew 1:1-16

LATER YEARS

VALENTINE FLOWER

So many Valentines ago
you sent me many flowers,
tokens of a simple love
so recently new-born.

I give just one to let you know
that after many years and hours
you're still my one and only love
when night fades to each dawn.

Sometimes the way was hard and slow,
but sun came through the showers.
In every passing trial that love
has never waxed forlorn.

So as the years may come and go,
no matter what the alien powers
may we find always that our love
will weather every storm.

WHERE GOD IS

Holy places, sacred spaces –
there I meet with God.
In the sunlight, sometimes shadows,
He will always wait for me.

In simple church or great cathedral
God will make His presence known.
In a park, or field, or garden
Nature tells me "He is here!"

In the street or in my study
He transforms the place I'm at.
With head in book when travelling
He's in the pages, crisp and clear.

Holy places, sacred spaces –
God may fashion every one.
Thin place, broad road, narrow path,
He changes our environment.

Dark place, light space, grey or bright,
God will shed His healing glow.
Sad place, dull space, cold and damp,
He will warm us with His love.

In life's noise of war and bloodshed,
times when fear pervades the world,
we may seek that tiny crevice
where God's presence may be found.

Space for peace and place of refuge,
we can never be alone
when, though, strangers without rest,
He is all the space we need.

THREADS OF LIFE*

My life's become a garment, wearing thin,
each thread an anniversary
I kept, or lost in travelling -
some places five, at others ten or more.
Some threads are golden, others merely tin –
a diamond traces out the threads of faith
and failure, stitches dropped or torn.

The silver threads and rubies faded fast –
birth, rebirth, commitment
lengthened out my days
until the Jubilate turned to tears
at times and places torn apart,
then gaping holes displayed
the fabric of my heart.

This year, next year,
ten years from a passing,
sixty for new life -
and fifty threads of love
that tied the knot.

* This poem was included in a Wedding Anniversary card.

DIAMOND DAY*

Forbid it, Lord, that I should glory –
save in the Cross ...

The words have echoed down the years
to this, my Diamond Day,
when I recall the pledge I made
to serve you to the end.

The Bible said it was to be
the moment my life changed,
when I lived no longer for myself
but in your service, Lord.

You are the Way, the Truth, the Life –
those were the words I heard.
But sixty years have passed now –
Lord, where has that way led?

I gave myself to you that night –
next day you gifted me;
but what, Lord, have I done for you
who did so much for me?

Yes, I have tried to serve you
who freed me from much pain,
and set me on a good road,
yet still I went astray.

You gave me love and comfort,
a home to call my own –
a family, friends and ministry –
I don't deserve them all.

I squandered your best gift, Lord –
sometimes I let it die,
forgotten or misused so oft'
when barriers arose.

I gave in much to enmity –
the ones who blocked your call
and left me unfulfilled for you –
I still forgave them all.

And yet I know I failed you,
and now it's far too late
to heed the call you gave me –
I still search for my place.

I sought to work through others,
enabled many more
to do the things I longed to do,
I felt that I was made for.

Only at the last, Lord,
as I stand before your throne
shall I know what I've accomplished
or how miserably I've failed.

I've missed those opportunities
You set within my way.
Lord, how greatly I'm repenting
on this, my Diamond Day.

* Written in Hull on 8th April 2015, the sixtieth anniversary of my Christian commitment, and based on Galatians 6:14.

GOLDEN DAY*

Did we, those fifty years ago
anticipate the coming day
when gold would mean more than a day
of snow white dress,
flowers, cake or even rings,
but time lived out in company,
moving growing, travelling on
through storm and tempest,
times of grief
and sometimes just a glimpse of peace.

The road was rough,
not paved with gold,
but what is life if ever smooth
and comfort comes too easily?
It's so much greater accolade
that we have companied this far,
that God has given us grace to be
true to each other, faithfully
and true to Him whose gift we are –
we thank Him for our Golden Day.

* Written on our Golden Wedding Anniversary, 17th July 2015, at the Victoria Lodge Hotel, Leamington Spa.

ALL THE WAY

I can't remember my first steps,
my infancy's a blur;
first day at school a nightmare –
what was I doing there?

Growing up was difficult,
making friends so hard.
In the middle of a Nowhere
so many holds were barred.

I longed so much for freedom
but hopes and dreams seemed dead
till one day I met Jesus
with him my misery fled.

That day he turned my life around –
I was alone no more.
He befriended and then gifted me
from his enormous store.

But still so many obstacles
seemed thrust upon my way.
Harsh realities of living
beset me day by day.

I knew he was beside me
through everyone I lost,
yet moving on along the road
each new stage came with cost.

His gifts to me are priceless –
I value them so much.
On every lonely pathway
I've sensed that tender touch.

It causes me to stop awhile,
to ponder and to pray
for no matter where I've wandered
He's been with me all the way.

Now that I'm old and looking back
it's much easier to see
the times when I lost faith in God
though He kept faith with me.

Dare I now look ahead and ask
what future years will bring?
I've walked with Him for sixty years –
and we're still travelling.

ONE WORLD

One world we have –
just one within a universe
of vacant worlds.

It is enough if we are kind,
respect and nurture it
as if it were a precious jewel
all our own!

THREE-QUARTERS OF A CENTURY*

Three-quarters of a century –
    and how the world has changed!
    Its songs come ever-louder,
    fast-paced rhythms pulsing out
sweeping all before them
at its mechanistic stage.

Three-quarters of a century –
    and how you too have changed –
    but hope-filled songs of yesterday
    still echo in your heart
and urge you on regardless
of this socialistic age.

Three-quarters of a century –
    and now time's changing pace –
    earth's music seems much softer
    as it fills a smaller space;
yet still strikes notes of wonder
in this technologic age.

* A greeting for my husband's seventy-fifth birthday.

THE WRONG TURNING*

How often has my life taken a wrong turning?
Even blindly following a spiritual SatNav is no guarantee
of reaching my final destination
if I ignore the warning signs en route -
the diversion set there for my safety,
preventing me from wildly breezing into danger –
the floods, the road-works, falling rocks, dead ends
that life throws up to thwart the unexpected.

So often on a precipice I've had to halt
because a staying hand has barred my way
and turned me back to safety,
or some intrusion stopped me sinking without trace.
One time a lack of fear sent me tumbling in a road
as a monster lorry slammed its brakes.
(My mother never knew!)
My neighbour not so fortunate –
but still I never learnt.

It's hard to learn the lessons of life's travel,
the times that should be spent applying rules –
forgetting that the Spirit-life
is no less fraught with danger
than crossing a main road against the lights.

* Written during an ArtServe Conference at The Hayes, Swanwick.

ROOTS REVISITED

I went back to my childhood home
to contemplate my roots.
The day was dull and wet and bleak,
no friendly face with whom to speak:
I buried them.

Another year a random bus
tempted me on board.
The day was bright, it promised good.
I travelled back again to brood
my unforgotten past.

I wandered through the village street,
marking every change;
came to the church and there I found
class-mates' names carved all around,
left for posterity.

The memories flooded back to me
of solace in those hallowed walls
at times when I was very sad,
when good things faded into bad –
a lonely child.

Across the road my treasured school
transforming to a house.
There I my pent-up anger vent
reaped reward in punishment
I well deserved.

Beside the village pond I wept
for those I'd loved and lost,
where desperate love-sick frogs each year
created carnage everywhere –
Such memories!

The place and I had both moved on –
I no more felt I could belong,
but still I knew some unseen force
subconsciously would steer my course
and draw me back –
and back again.

TIME FLIES

Time was when we would wander far,
through bluebell woods and primrose ways,
the laughing stones we stumbled on,
the daffodils that waved us by,
white garlic pungent by the weir.

Time was less precious then than now,
when more than fifty years have gone,
We must now seize each moment as it comes
for time is swift, flies fast away.

THE SECRET OF THE CHAPEL*
A True [Unfinished] Story

A lonely little chapel
stands high upon a hill.
Its doors are locked, its worship done,
the organ damp and still.

It has stood there like a beacon
almost two hundred years.
It holds so many secrets
of life and love and tears.

The time had come to let it go
and find another role.
No one now came to care for it,
the mildew took its toll.

But then one day a mystery
appeared to suggest
that near a tablet raised on high
a man was laid to rest.

His name was George, the minister
from Eighteen-fifty-four.
It seemed he had been buried
somewhere beneath the door.

That chapel all at once became
the place of interest.
We kept on going back to put
our theories to the test.

A garden rose behind the church,
a strip beneath the wall.
Uneven flagstones paved the court,
but no grave sign at all.

He was not found beneath the door
nor anywhere in sight.
No other record of his death
has ever come to light.

We've taken up the floorboards,
we've trawled the Ancestry,
but Brother George's whereabouts
remain a mystery.

And so we wonder, watch and wait
against its resurrection day.
What will it be, what will be found?
If only I could say!

* This refers to a former Primitive Methodist Chapel in a Derbyshire village.

THE LAST CHRISTMAS*
Requiem for the High Street

They try to make it look like Christmas:
bells, baubles and artificial trees -
but once vibrant stores
are filled with empty space,
white and bare,
shrouded in barriers,
ready to die.

Where there is life
the doom of unsold merchandise
reflects the tone –
prices slashed to bare reality.
A House in mourning
before its dying day.

Saved? Not saved
but squandered asset
stripped of all identity
its former glory pared away
to time without a future
in another year.

Walk through worn doors,
the white paint scuffed and grey,
into a high street fast reflecting
the gloom no sun can satisfy.
Dying cities filled with sadness
none can heal.

Time has moved on too fast –
its human touch and tenderness
lost in ether, air and anonymity -
a fast expanding universe
of technicality
accessed through ipads
not by pen
or even telephone.

"We must not give ourselves away.
We need no space in space
nor in a crowded high street,
still less a special store
with real humans offering to serve.
The server on the internet
is all we need."

Only when it's banished into history
will one survey the relics once so proud
and reminisce at such discarded space
trying to remember what was there,
what life was like ...

Just yesterday
the high street was a different place
that no one will remember.

* Written in the House of Fraser Store Café in Exeter.

EPIPHANY 2019

The Twelfth Day:
Day of gifts.
Gift day from our Loving God.
Day for giving
and forgiving,
for making promises –
our Covenant with God
to give and Be
for Him
Whose Gift is priceless
and eternal.

This day
and every day
are gifts
for giving
all to God
through others.

EASTER DAY 2020*

No daffodils to decorate the cross
or sacrament to celebrate new life –
just virtual worship via video links,
an *agape* for coffee-time,
all engineered by technology.

No sunrise services, high on some hill,
first Easter eggs to follow in their wake.
No special breakfasts linking times of praise
or alleluias ringing round the town –
the streets are almost vacant now.

In Bethlehem the tomb stands empty still –
no tourists flock to gape and disbelieve.
No journeying on the Via Dolorosa
or sharing pain at Calvary's cruel hill.
A lonely Easter message at St. Mark's.

We look for hope, new life, a meaning
to the times we face today.
How glean the Easter message full of joy
when doom is surging all around
and death stalks every corridor?

So we must raise our heads and scan the scene,
take in the blossoms on the trees,
the flowers, not cut but growing vibrantly;
hear the mating calls of amorous birds
and welcome every creature in our midst.

For this is God's domain where nature thrives
in spite of fear and pestilence abroad.
Take in our lesson from contented cats,
be warmed by sunshine streaming through each branch,
and then believe one day we shall be free.

* Written at Hasland during the Coronavirus pandemic when churches were closed, even on Easter Sunday. An *agape* is a love-feast traditionally comprising a simple meal of bread and water.

EIGHT DECADES

July 2020

Seventy-nine!
To think I've been here on earth for almost eighty years –
more – much more – than half my life!
Where has it gone?
Flown like a bird losing its way?
What has it done?
So little, it seems, to show –
but maybe that is something
I'm just not meant to know.

It was not my life alone –
I gave myself to God, Who in His good time
gave me another –
and then two more, for whom I had to care.
And finally one more, less willingly perhaps –
a quarter of my life on tenterhooks!

What has life given me in return?
A sense of place, in many places –
homes and friends – and yet
heartaches and rejection by the score;
these things to bear for they were human-made
and not from God, as some would have me think.

Who saw me through?
God alone, who gave me family – and love –
such love of friends, especially those
who'd been rejected too
or knew me better than I knew
myself,
and loved me just the same.

I came into this world through fear –
how could I know that at the time
as that same fear dogged my childhood path,
measured in unhappiness and questioning
my need to be?

God rescued me – and gave me this one gift
I almost threw away –
but all through life, its troubles and regrets
this stays with me – and now
He tells me, "Share it, give it, for it speaks of Me."

What now my purpose going on?
He will reveal it, day by day
as I must trust and no more be afraid
or treasure sense of worthlessness
before the world.
There must be more for me to give and do – and be –
I must trust on, give thanks
and face eternity.

MEMORIES OF JAFFA*

I see you in my dreams, at my side –
a fleeting glimpse, a ginger flash
and then you're gone.
I open a door,
peep round the corner, expectantly –
the space on the bed is vacant now.

Sometimes I hear the plaintive sound,
'Let me in' – but no one's there;
a howl of discontent,
silent pleading on a window sill
or the rumbling of affection
as you sneak closer to my heart –
you loved me once.

Your pleading eyes begging a comforting embrace
would be so welcome now
when I recall rejection at the last,
remembering how you stole away
endearingly to others,
in your pain.

You didn't understand tough love
that yearned too much for you to stay
and make you well;
or that I didn't mete the savagery
that cut you down before your time.

I turn, this way and that
and see the corners where you fled for sanctuary
and broke my helpless heart.
I see your image on a hundred snaps
roll across a screen
and want those days again
that ceased when you were lost to me.

Are you now at peace,
deep in the garden corner,
safe under snowy blanket
where forget-me-nots refused to grow –
memorials of others
now become a memory of you?

* Jaffa, our fourth and last cat (pictured on the front cover), died on 15th December 2020.

CHRISTMAS IS OVER*

Christmas is over – a one-day event
on the calendar of confusion.
Now the real business of living and not living resumes –
with a burning question –
When?

When will that one day return
and become again the pattern of our lives –
days of friendship, fellowship and fun –
holding hands and comforting?
Life can never be the same -
too much – too many – lost,
so many suffering – or afraid.
What is the ground of all this fear?
Loss of friends, family – self?
Fear of passing on from this life to the next?
Fear of what will come because of what is past?
How we have lived determining how we die?
Fear of death itself?
The pain of waiting, wondering,
praying for some miracle to come our way
and save us from this time of trial?

That one day gave us pause –
now it has gone.
Christmas is over –
          or has it just begun?

* Reflecting on Christmas Day 2020.

ACKNOWLEDGMENTS

The first person I must thank for his help with the onerous task of short-listing the final selection is Geoffrey, my husband of nearly 56 years, whose 80th birthday falls just a month before mine, so in a sense we were truly in it together. He has not always appreciated my poetic greetings for his special days but he has an eye for what he calls *real* poetry; that helped to ensure a balance of styles and content which was very helpful.

My thanks also to Patrick Mancini of Moorleys who was willing to take me on once again, despite my pre-lockdown promise that there would be no more books! Also to Oonagh Robinson and Tracey Dean for their helpful comments and for dealing with my idiosyncrasies. I greatly value and rely on their expertise in producing such an attractive finished product.

Lastly, to all the friends I've made over the years in my various activities from editing books to selling them to publishing them, and to others with whom I've worked in the many enterprises I've undertaken or been involved with, and especially those friends who have been with me (generally now via snail mail) from my college and early working days. I've lost and mourn many over the years so treasure those who can now celebrate with us during this milestone year. This book is for all of you – with love and thanks.

Previous Publications

[All Cottage Books or PBP unless otherwise stated]

Messages of Devon [1991]
Occult: The Hidden Dangers [with Margaret Oxenham 1991]
Aspects of the Sermon [1993]
Farewell to Wincolmlee [1994]
Time and The Gospel [1995]
Adhering to the Rules [1995, Areopagus 2000]
Fish-cakes and Fantasy [The Winterton Lecture 1996]
Something to Rhyme About [Ed. with Daphne Ayles, 1996]
Letters to The Editor ... [1997]
A World of Love [1997]
Memo to God [1998]
Still Dancing [1998]
Candles in the Darkness [1998]
In Debt to C. S. Lewis [On the influence of his fiction, 1999]
Candles in Draughty Spaces [chapbook 1999]
Fifty Days [2000]
Meeting Jesus [Ed. 2000]
Happy in Hospital [Ed. with Daphne Ayles, 2000]
Lenten Light [2001]
Penitential Tears [2001]
Constantine – with Care! [As Annette Collins, Fiction 2001]
Daughters of Eve [Feather Books 2001]

Publications in Print

[All by Moorleys]

Prayers for Worship [1997, reprinted 2020]
More Prayers for Worship [2009]
The Bound Lamb and Other Reflections [2013, reprinted 2020]
Reflections on a Journey [2017]
For Many Occasions ... [2018]
Advent Women [2018]

The past, all that I really am, goes with me into the future.